ALL NEW PEOPLE

BY ZACH BRAFF

★

★

DRAMATISTS
PLAY SERVICE
INC.

ALL NEW PEOPLE
Copyright © 2012, Zach Braff

All Rights Reserved

SPECIAL NOTE

SPECIAL NOTE ON SONGS AND RECORDINGS

ALL NEW PEOPLE received its world premiere at Second Stage Theatre (Carole Rothman, Artistic Director; Casey Reitz, Executive Director) in New York City on July 25, 2011. It was directed by Peter DuBois; the set design was by Alexander Dodge; the costume design was by Bobby Frederick Tilley II; the lighting design was by Japhy Weideman; the sound design was by M. L. Dogg; the projection design was by Aaron Rhyne; and the production stage manager was Lori Ann Zepp. The cast was as folllows:

CHARLIE . . . . Justin Bartha
EMMA . . . . Krysten Ritter
MYRON . . . . David Wilson Barnes
KIM . . . . Anna Camp

CHARACTERS

CHARLIE

EMMA

KIM

MYRON

PLACE

A high-end Long Beach Island, New Jersey beach house.

TIME

The dead of winter.

ALL NEW PEOPLE

*Great upbeat music plays as the audience filters in. A scrim
covers the stage. A record player sits downstage of the scrim with
various records next to it. As the house lights go down:
Something like the song "The Buzzards of Bourbon Street" by
Gaelic Storm kicks in loud.* The scrim rises to reveal Charlie,
35, standing on a chair with an extension cord fashioned as a
noose around his neck. He smokes a cigarette.*

*We're in a high-end Long Beach Island, New Jersey beach
house. It is the dead of winter. We see snow outside the windows.
An unlit fireplace is stage right. On a downbeat of the song,
lights are full up and the music changes to sound as though it's
coming from a stereo in the home.*

*Charlie looks for a place to ash his cigarette, but realizes his
reach is limited by the noose. He stretches as far as he can for
the ashtray on a nearby counter and tosses it in.*

*Suddenly, Charlie hears the "bwoop-woop-woop" of a car
alarm being turned on. His eyes register his confusion; "Who
the fuck could that be?"*

EMMA. *(Offstage.)* All right then, Mr. Goldberg; well, I just got
to the house and I'll put all the lights on for you and get the heat
started so you'll be able to have a look at the place without freezing
yourselves … great, and you have the directions? All right, see you
in a bit. *(Charlie wrestles with what to do. Just as he begins to try and
loosen the cord from around his neck … Emma enters bundled up. She
sees Charlie.)* Oh my God! *(In a scramble to get the noose off of him,*

Charlie loses his footing on the chair and knocks it over. He begins flailing around, swinging from the noose.) Oh my GOD! Oh my GOD! *(Emma runs over and picks up the chair and helps Charlie steer his legs back onto it.)* Oh my God! What the fuck is wrong with you?! What the fuck is wrong with you?!

CHARLIE. Who the fuck are you?!

EMMA. Who the hell are you and why are you trying to kill yourself in the middle of one of my summer rentals?!

CHARLIE. This is my parents' beach house. You have no right to just barge in here without knocking.

EMMA. It's the middle of winter at the beach! No one's s'posed to be here. I'm trying to rent the place for your parents! I certainly didn't think anybody was gonna be in here trying to hang themselves! To *Riverdance* music!

CHARLIE. I'm not trying to hang myself!

EMMA. Really?! Just going for a little swing then? Just gonna dangle by your neck for a bit and think things over?

CHARLIE. Would you please just get the fuck out of here?!

EMMA. No, I will not! You know, you might start off with a brief thank you to me for saving your life.

CHARLIE. I didn't ask to be saved. What I want, is some fucking privacy!

EMMA. Look, I don't wanna be insensitive.

CHARLIE. Try a little harder.

EMMA. I have no idea what's going on with you or what your current situation is. It does seem a bit like you might be trying to hang yourself with an extension cord, but I'm fully aware that things aren't always what they seem to be: never judge a book by its cover and all that. You may very well have been trying to ... wire up some Christmas lights when you ... tripped and got all tangled up in that extension cord. But if I don't rent a house for next summer soon, I'm gonna be fired and they're gonna try to send me back to bloody fucking England because I don't have a green card or a visa and there aren't too many jobs I can get. Pretty soon I'll be right up there with you, accidentally hanging myself. So would you please do a stranger a tiny kindness before you die and allow me to attempt to rent your parents' ridiculously expensive beach house to this nice Jewish couple Miriam and Irving Goldberg. Please, fucker, I'm begging you. *(He stares at her a beat. Lights a cigarette.)*

CHARLIE. Go ahead.

EMMA. Thank you. *(She sits there. After a beat.)*
CHARLIE. Well, where are they?
EMMA. They're not here yet. They said they were on their way. But they're old and Jewish; it could be hours. They said they had to first pick up their grandson, Saul. Why Saul needs to come, I have no idea. Personally, I think they're gonna try and set me up with him. With Saul, a dentist. A dentist who does community theater. He probably wears *Les Mis* T-shirts to the gym. Jesus Christ, do you mind if I have a drink? *(Before he can answer, she pulls a liquor bottle out of her purse and takes a swig.)* I'm sorry, I'm being completely insensitive and bloody fucking selfish. I suck at being human; desperation has made me evil. So I apologize … New chapter: Why were you trying to off yourself? And why hanging; it seems to be the most aggressive of all methods. Haven't you any pills?
CHARLIE. I have pills.
EMMA. Really. What have you got?
CHARLIE. Xanax, Valium, Klonopin.
EMMA. Party, party, party. We could turn this day around for both of us real quick, couldn't we? I'm just kidding. Well, not really; but that's irrelevant. Back to you … What put you over the edge?
CHARLIE. I really don't wanna talk about it.
EMMA. Well, what's the point in being coy about it now? If you're gonna do it, you're gonna do it, right? They always say that people who really wanna do themselves in are gonna find a way. *(Realizing.)* Maybe God sent you me and the Goldbergs for one last shot at talking you out of it. Don't you believe in fate? I'm sorry, what's your name?
CHARLIE. Charlie.
EMMA. Don't you believe in fate, Charlie? Here you are, in an empty beach house, on a deserted island, in the middle of the fucking winter, moments away from ending it all, when in I walk. Does that give you no pause? Maybe God sent me to provide you with some sort of … access to the doors of your mind that remain rusted closed. *(Beat.)* Sorry. I should tell you that I am super-stoned right now. So if I say silly nonsense like that, you're gonna have to forgive me.
CHARLIE. Sure. Look, I …
EMMA. You want me to go.
CHARLIE. You seem like you're a very nice person —
EMMA. Really?
CHARLIE. No; and I don't wanna be rude …

EMMA. But you've got things to do … Hmmm. You know you've put me into a smidgen of a moral conundrum here; you do realize that, Charlie. I don't think I can leave.

CHARLIE. And why is that?

EMMA. I think I may have been sent here to help. You may believe that or not, depending on where you stand on God and fate and destiny and all that; it's none of my business. But I do know that it's a little bizarre I walked in when I did, since I wasn't even gonna show them this house because it's outside their price range. This morning they called up and asked to see it. Out of the blue. Spooky. A religious person might think God intervened. I don't know what you believe, but … Jesus or Moses or Mohammed, Vishnu, who's the one with the arms? The elephant with all the arms?

CHARLIE. Ganesh.

EMMA. Ganesh. I doubt it was Ganesh; kind of a simple assignment for a god with so many arms. But whomever your god is, I think may have channeled an intervention through two cranky old Jews from the Newark suburbs. I think I'm here to help. So why did you tie a noose around your neck, my new friend?

CHARLIE. To put it as simply as possible: I'm not happy.

EMMA. Who is? Have you ever met *anyone* that's happy for longer than fifteen minutes every once in a while? If they told you they were, they were full of shit. Who told you you were owed happiness?

CHARLIE. I don't think I'm owed anything.

EMMA. A man gives his child a million dollars and says, "Son, this is everything I've worked for, go enjoy your life." The kid comes back the next day and says, "Thanks for the million, Dad, but I'd also like a fucking robot sidekick." Is that kid a dick?

CHARLIE. What the fuck are you talking about?

EMMA. Isn't that *you?* You're the dickhead kid asking for a robot sidekick when you've already gotten a million dollars. God gave you life and you've come back to whine for happiness. Life should be enough. Take life and walk … be grateful.

CHARLIE. Okay, look, I know you're a little out of sorts, so I'm gonna say this as simply as possible. I don't give a fuck about God. Now, I suppose it's obvious, I've got a couple things on my mind. But don't you fucking dare stroll in here and just splatter your religion all over the room, okay? *(A cell phone rings.)*

EMMA. You know I'm not really sure what the etiquette is in this situation. Should I not get that?

8

CHARLIE. Go ahead.

EMMA. Normally I wouldn't; and I agree with you that it's a little weird because of the nature of what you're sharing. But the truth is, I'm expecting an important delivery and this pertains to that.

CHARLIE. Go ahead. *(She answers. Attempts to be covert.)*

EMMA. Hello? … Myron; thank God. Look; can you come by the big house in Loveladies? Well, I came over here to show these people the house and it turns out someone's trying to hang himself in the living room … No, I'm not shitting you … Yes, I have to get this all sorted out before they arrive; I think it will be a bit hard for them to imagine playing Jenga in the summertime if they think there's some suicidal ghost swinging over their heads … *(She notices Charlie staring at her.)* Okay, I should go. *(She hangs up. He stares at her.)* You know, even as I said that I realized it was crass. That was my friend, Myron.

CHARLIE. Awesome.

EMMA. So you were saying …

CHARLIE. I wasn't saying anything. Look, would you mind terribly waiting outside for your friend?

EMMA. It's freezing outside! I can be quiet. I won't say another word.

CHARLIE. I don't think that's possible.

EMMA. No. I can do that.

CHARLIE. I'm pretty sure you can't. I'd literally bet my life on it.

EMMA. We could have like a meditation.

CHARLIE. No meditation. Just quiet. No talking. You'll just wait for your friend in silence. You'll get whatever he's delivering and then be off on your merry little way.

EMMA. No. You're right. Peace and fucking quiet. Amen. I talk too much when I'm nervous. Sorry … I don't know why I'm so nervous … I mean, I know why I am, I suppose, the circumstances are … unique. But I can handle it.

CHARLIE. Okay.

EMMA. I just can't quite … stop … talking.

CHARLIE. Okay, well … let's start now.

EMMA. Yes. I agree. *(Emma paces a bit. It's clear silence is hard for her. She looks at photos, then crosses to a piece of African art that sits on a stand behind the couch. It consists of hundreds of tiny beads woven together. She fondles it, and almost immediately the beads begin to fall all over the floor, making a ton of noise and destroying the artwork. When it finally stops, they both stare at each other.)* I can fix that.

CHARLIE. Just please leave it.

EMMA. Don't be silly, it won't take long. I'm just gonna need some thread and a magnifying glass.

CHARLIE. Please just leave it.

EMMA. No, no, no. This is so embarrassing. I'll have my friend Myron come in and help me fix it. He's good with the arts and all that; taught high school drama for ten years. Watches tons of movies. He's completely in love with me and I may have to marry him to stay in the country, but talk about a last resort; I have absolutely no attraction to him sexually, but I love his mind. He's one of those people who so beautifully straddles the line of insane and sane. *(Beat.)* Maybe *that's* your problem.

CHARLIE. I'm insane?

EMMA. You're *too* sane. Insane, you'd be walking around Manhattan yelling at pigeons and talking to statues — I once watched a homeless guy in Union Square Park have a thirty-minute heated discussion with a statue of Gandhi. Just screaming at fucking Gandhi! Telling him to eat a fucking sandwich. And no one's doing anything. Not one person in that park had Gandhi's back except me. So I walked right up to him and said, "Listen, you crazy fuck! Leave Ghandi alone. Have some respect! He was a man of peace. If he wanted to eat, he'd eat." He called me a cunt and roller-bladed off. Anyway, my point is, you're not that kind of crazy. You're probably too sane. You think too much; that'll drive you crazy.

CHARLIE. Has anyone ever told you that you talk a lot?

EMMA. Yes. But I feel I was born with just so much to say.

CHARLIE. What is your name?

EMMA. Emma.

CHARLIE. Charlie.

EMMA. Yes I know. Sad Charlie. It's nice to meet you. And just in time too, huh?

CHARLIE. Emma, I killed six people.

EMMA. What's that now?

CHARLIE. That's why I'm gonna kill myself. I murdered six innocent people. You asked what put me over the edge ... the straw that broke the camel's back ... It was that. That's what it was. *(Silence.)* You have less to say now.

EMMA. That's a pretty heavy piece of straw, sad Charlie. You're not gonna murder me, are you?

CHARLIE. I haven't decided yet. *(The doorbell rings.)*

EMMA. Oh, fuck. The Goldbergs! *(Beat.)* Would you mind terribly not mentioning this to them? Something tells me this whole … murder/suicide situation might turn them off the house a bit. *(She drapes the noose against the wall and looks at it.)* That's actually quite decorative. *(She quickly crosses to the door. She opens it to reveal Myron. He is in his late thirties and wears a fireman's uniform.)* Welcome!

MYRON. Hey, baby.

EMMA. Oh, Myron, it's just you. Thank God … Come on in. This is Charlie; this is his parents' house.

MYRON. No, it isn't. This isn't your house.

CHARLIE. How do you know?

MYRON. Because I know a lot of things.

EMMA. You said this was your house.

CHARLIE. I did say that.

MYRON. This is Kevin O'Donnell's house. Super-rich stock-broker guy. That's not you. Sweetheart, how do you not know whose house you're renting out?

EMMA. Our office handles over a thousand houses on this island, Myron. Do you think I've got everybody's family memorized? Do I look like the fucking *Lion King*?

MYRON. Elephants are the ones with good memories, not lions.

EMMA. Whatever.

CHARLIE. He's right.

EMMA. About the lions?

CHARLIE. No. Kevin's my friend. This is his house. Are you a fireman?

MYRON. No, I'm a gay stripper. What's with the noose?

EMMA. Charlie's planning on killing himself.

MYRON. Fuck, that's right! Exciting. I was just sitting at the station staring at the wall. This is already better.

EMMA. And one more thing, Myron … moments ago he also told me he killed some people.

MYRON. Emma, are you stoned?

EMMA. You have no idea.

MYRON. This guy hasn't killed anybody. He's fucking with you.

CHARLIE. You just met me. How could you possibly know what I'm capable of? How do you know I'm not seconds away from blowing your fucking head off?

MYRON. I'm a vibe guy, okay? I get vibes. And your vibe, frankly, reeks of pussy. I think you're making shit up to try to get laid. And

11

there's nothing wrong with that; I do it all the time. Last week I told some girl in Atlantic City I was at the Normandy invasion. Now that would have made me at least 89 years old, but she bought it. She blew me behind a shoe-shine booth outside Caesars; said it was "for the troops."

EMMA. What a lovely story.

MYRON. The next night I even upped the ante: pretended to have a nightmare and started yelling, "The gooks are coming, the gooks are coming!" That drove her crazy. So I've played this game; I know how it works.

CHARLIE. The Japanese weren't at Normandy.

MYRON. What?

CHARLIE. Amongst all the preposterous nonsense that you just said, one phrase stands out amongst the rest as the most idiotic. You implied that the Japanese were at Normandy. It was the Germans. The Americans called them "Jerry," but there were no "gooks."

MYRON. No gooks at Normandy?

CHARLIE. No gooks at Normandy.

EMMA. That sounds like the title of some brave general's biography … How many people did you say you killed, Charlie?

CHARLIE. Six.

MYRON. Bullshit.

CHARLIE. I think I'm gonna have a drink now. *(As Charlie crosses to the bar, he slips on the hundreds of beads that have been scattered across the floor from the artwork. He lands on his back.)* Awwww, fuck!

EMMA. Oh my God! Charlie! The beads! Are you okay? You are just not having a good day, are you?

MYRON. *(Suddenly suspicious.)* This place has been booby-trapped. I saw this in a movie once …

EMMA. *Home Alone.*

MYRON. Yes. *Home Alone.*

EMMA. It has not been booby-trapped. I broke some African art. It was a piece of shit anyway; probably made in China. The beads went everywhere, I need your help sewing it all back together. *(Charlie stands holding his back.)*

MYRON. That's gonna hurt tomorrow.

EMMA. Luckily for Charlie there won't be a tomorrow. I suppose that's *some* good news. *(Charlie pours a drink at the bar.)*

MYRON. I'll take one of those too, thanks.

CHARLIE. I'm not pouring you a drink; you're a fireman. What if there's a fire? *(Emma and Myron laugh.)* What's so funny?

EMMA. It's the dead of winter, Charlie. There aren't gonna be any fires.

CHARLIE. Things don't burn in the winter?

MYRON. They do, but they don't. There's no one on the island. Only a few thousand people in the off-season. Almost two hundred thousand in the height of summer. But right now, this place is a ghost town. Anybody who's here now, is here 'cause they got no place else to go.

EMMA. Guilty as charged. I'd love to be anywhere else but here. No offense to my only friend; but I'm stuck. Outta money, no visa, can't rent a house to save my life … I'm hopelessly tangled in nothingness.

MYRON. I mean there are the occasional things, of course … smoke alarm at the coffee shop, somebody tries to make a fire and forgets to open the flue. But for the most part, it's quiet around here. I can have a drink … or three.

EMMA. Myron does other things in the off-season.

CHARLIE. Like what?

EMMA. Myron's the island's drug dealer.

MYRON. I prefer "Purveyor of Distractions."

CHARLIE. Okay, look. I have a gun in the other room. And if you people don't get up off that couch and get the fuck out of here right now, I'm gonna go in there and when I come back out, I'm gonna blow your fucking heads off!

EMMA. Myron? What are your vibes telling you about this latest outburst?

MYRON. They're telling me his gun's probably orange and says "Super Soaker" on the side.

EMMA. Why would you want to kill your friends, Charlie? I think Myron and I might be the only friends you've got. There isn't exactly a line out the door of people trying to stop you from turning yourself into a human piñata. Isn't that right, Myron?

MYRON. Now he's got a gun. I think he's just trying to get into your Underoos by weaving some kinda Bonnie and Clyde crime caper. I think, she caught you trying to dangle yourself and you thought, "Hey, I might as well go out with a bang … " So all of a sudden you're a killer on the run. I call bullshit, I think you just wanna get in her pants by titillating her with fancy tales of stealing her all sorts of diamonds and bonds …

CHARLIE. Bonds?

MYRON. Whatever they steal from banks these days …

CHARLIE. I think it's still cash.

MYRON. In the movie *Beverly Hills Cop* they stole bonds.

EMMA. I really just want a green card. Can you steal me that, Charlie? I'll be Bonnie to your Clyde if I could just have a bloody green card. *(The action on stage freezes. A scrim quickly flies in, covering the entire proscenium. A pre-shot film flickers to life on the panels. A pub in London: Emma sits across from Badger, a tough-looking British man.)*

BADGER. Hand me the envelope. *(She does.)* It'll be done on Monday; the day before he's scheduled to be paroled. You need to leave the country. No contact with anyone you know.

EMMA. I can't even call my dad? I have to say goodbye …

BADGER. Never again. No email, not even a postcard.

EMMA. Is that it then?

BADGER. There is one more thing. Clementine Thomas, nicknamed "Emma" by her mother, Annabelle, who died of breast cancer when her only daughter was barely eight years old. Your only surviving relative is your father, Russel, who tends bar at the Lion's Head pub in Camden. He roots for Tottenham Hotspur and likes to feed ducks in Regent's Park after church on Sunday morning.

EMMA. How do you know all this? What's your point?

BADGER. We never met. You've never seen me. If you *do* ever see me again; it's because you fucked up. You done something wrong. And I'll slit your father's fucking throat with a samurai sword I won at auction without raising my pulse even one half a beat for the minute. You get all that?

EMMA. Yes.

BADGER. *(He sings sweetly.)* Oh my darlin', oh my darlin', oh my darlin' Clementine, you are lost and gone forever, dear sweet darlin' Clementine. Put your tray table up, Emma Thomas; we're about to get going. *(The scrim flies out, lights up onstage.)*

CHARLIE. You can't steal a green card.

MYRON. You could if you put the right team together.

CHARLIE. What?

MYRON. You know those movies where they have to assemble the right team and everyone has their specialty and in the end it all works out because they each did their part?

CHARLIE. Yeah.

MYRON. Well, I'll bet if you put the right team together, you could steal Emma a green card.

EMMA. Ooh, please put a team together, Charlie. I wanna follow the American dream and collect unemployment.

CHARLIE. I am not a thief!

EMMA. "You can be anything you wanna be"; that's what Dad always said.

CHARLIE. I don't know anything about putting a team of thieves together. I've never stolen anything in my life. *(Beat.)* I'm a fighter pilot for the U.S. Air Force. *(Silence.)* I fly the F-22 Raptor for the Air Force! I've flown over two hundred sorties over Iraq and Afghanistan. I'm a fighter pilot. I'm not a fucking thief.

MYRON. Wow. That's a whole 'nother level. Do you mind if I use that one?

CHARLIE. It's not a fucking pickup line, asshole. You're really starting to piss me off.

MYRON. You just don't strike me as a fighter pilot. You're a little too … Jewy.

CHARLIE. That makes absolutely no sense. The Israeli Air Force is the second-best air force in the world. I imagine there's probably a few Jews flying their planes. I'm not a liar.

EMMA. Well, technically you did lie about owning this house.

CHARLIE. Kevin O'Donnell and I went to college together. I told him I'm going through a hard time. I wanted to be alone, so he said I could come here.

EMMA. To kill yourself.

CHARLIE. He doesn't know about that part. The guy's got more money than anybody I know; he can afford to do his friend a favor.

MYRON. Well, the place is just sitting here …

CHARLIE. What?

MYRON. What I mean is … the house is just sitting here. It's the off-season.

EMMA. Myron, don't minimize Kevin's favor.

MYRON. I'm not minimizing his favor. It was very nice of him to let you off yourself in his beach house. But it's not like he's really given you anything at a loss to himself … What I mean is, he hasn't paid for anything.

EMMA. Heat …

MYRON. Yes, he's given you heat. How generous! *(The doorbell rings. They all freeze.)*

15

EMMA. Oh fuck! The Goldbergs!

CHARLIE. Jesus Christ.

EMMA. Okay. You two; just act like you're normal. *(She crosses to the window.)* Wait, there's no car … Myron, did you tell anyone you were coming here?

MYRON. No, but I mean … people know I'm here.

CHARLIE. How?

MYRON. 'Cause I got the fire truck parked outside.

CHARLIE. You parked the fucking fire truck in front of the house?

MYRON. Well, when I pulled up I didn't exactly expect this little fiesta, did I? I thought I was just dropping off some Canadian anti-depressants for "tea and crumpets" over there.

EMMA. For the record, they're not Canadian anti-depressants. They're produced here by the free and the brave. *(The doorbell rings again. Charlie tries to see who it is.)*

CHARLIE. Who the fuck is out there?! *(Myron has poured glue into a brown paper bag he has found in the kitchen. He begins to inhale and exhale the air in the bag.)* Are you huffing glue?!

MYRON. Yes, I am; glue calms me. Now why don't you go open door number one and see what we've won. I'm hoping it's a dining set! *(Emma opens the door. There stands Kim. She is 22 and stunning. They all stare. She looks at Myron in his uniform.)*

EMMA. Hello.

KIM. Is there a fire? *(Myron is dumbfounded by her beauty.)*

MYRON. Uhhh … not anymore. I put it out.

KIM. Oh. Thank God. I'm looking for Charlie Bloom.

CHARLIE. I'm Charlie.

KIM. Is everything okay?

CHARLIE. Yes, everything's fine. I'm sorry, but who are you? How did you know I was here?

KIM. Kevin O'Donnell sent me from New York City.

CHARLIE. To do what?

KIM. To cheer you up. He said you were down in the dumps. I'm a present. I'm yours for the night.

MYRON. Oh my God, we've won a prostitute.

KIM. I'm not a prostitute, I'm an escort.

MYRON. And I'm not a fireman, I'm a pressurized water courier. Come on inside. It's freezing out.

CHARLIE. Wait … *(She comes in the room. Myron closes the door and brings her into the room.)*

16

KIM. It smells like glue.

MYRON. We were making a collage.

KIM. Fun; I love crafts. Hi, I'm Kim.

MYRON. I'm Myron Dunlap, chief of the Long Beach Island Fire Department and personal concierge to all VIPs from the neighboring island of Manhattan.

KIM. Nice to meet you.

CHARLIE. You're the chief of the fire department?

MYRON. Yes. Why are you so surprised?

CHARLIE. Because you obviously have a drug problem!

MYRON. Doesn't really feel like a problem to me.

EMMA. Hello, I'm Emma. Welcome to our humble abode.

KIM. Cool. I like your accent.

EMMA. Thanks, I made it myself.

MYRON. Can I offer you a drink?

CHARLIE. No.

KIM. Sure, tequila's fine. Do you guys have any cocaine?

MYRON. Oh, I like the way you enter a party, young Kimberly. Allow me to send a quick text ...

EMMA. Get some nitrous oxide and a bag of Cheetos too. *(Myron takes out his phone and types a text.)*

CHARLIE. No, no, no, no. Stop taking your coat off. Look, I don't know how to say this nicely, but ... Get the fuck out! We are not having a party! Look ... ma'am ...

KIM. Kim.

CHARLIE. Kim. I'm really sorry, but I feel like there's been a misunderstanding. I can see what Kevin was trying to do. And he means well. But I'm not really in the mood to ...

KIM. You don't think I'm pretty?

MYRON. *I* think you're very pretty.

KIM. Thank you.

CHARLIE. What? No, you're very attractive. It's just that ...

EMMA. Charlie's having an off day; he's not really in the mood to be ... escorted.

KIM. Oh. Well, we don't have to really go anywhere. We can just sit here and talk if you want. Kevin bought me out for the whole night.

CHARLIE. The whole night? Look. It's not you ... it's me. I'm just — I'm going through kind of a tough time right now. I'm actually trying to remove the guests I currently have, so it does seem a bit counter-intuitive to be inviting new ones in.

KIM. Are you upset about the fire?

CHARLIE. The what, now?

KIM. Are you upset about the fire that he just put out?

CHARLIE. There was no fire.

MYRON. Eh, eh, eh … What he means is, to call it a fire would be an understatement. It was more like a mini-holocaust.

KIM. Oh. Where are all the other firemen?

CHARLIE. Yes, where are all the other firemen?

MYRON. Dead.

EMMA. Dead?

MYRON. Dead.

CHARLIE. Dead?

MYRON. Dead. She claimed them all.

KIM. You guys are fucking with me.

MYRON. Not yet, but we're looking forward to that.

CHARLIE. Listen, thanks for coming all the way down here, but I'm gonna have to take a rain check.

KIM. But I just let the car service go, and I drove three hours to get here. If you don't want me here, how am I supposed to get home?

MYRON. I can give you a lift.

KIM. In the fire truck.

MYRON. Of course.

CHARLIE. It's a great idea; why don't we get that going right now …

EMMA. But Myron; shouldn't you be grieving over all those dead men?

MYRON. You know, it really hasn't hit me yet. I imagine sometime tomorrow I'll throw on a little Sarah McLachlan and weep in the fetal position. But for now I just wanna be here with my close friends. Emma, Larry —

CHARLIE. Charlie.

MYRON. Charlie. And you: our new friend, Kim. Would you mind closing that door, Larry? It's freezing outside.

KIM. Listen, Charlie. Kevin bought me for you for the whole night … so I can't leave. I'm all yours. And you can do whatever you want to me, but between you and I, I'd appreciate it if you stayed away from my asshole.

EMMA. *(Emma's eyes go wide.)* Myron, could I have my Canadian anti-depressants now? I'm beginning to feel a downward spiral coming on.

KIM. Ooh what are you on? I take Celexa, Darvocet and the occasional Welbutrin for smoking. *(She lights a cigarette. Myron tosses a bottle of pills to Emma.)*

EMMA. Oh, mine don't really have a name. I'm an illegal alien, so I have to take what I can afford from our neighbor to the north. These ones are just labeled "Happier." I can't afford "Happiest."

KIM. It's funny, I would never have guessed you were Mexican. *(They all stare at her.)*

EMMA. Excuse me?

KIM. It's just your accent sounds so British — like Madonna's or Gwyneth Paltrow's. But you said you're an illegal alien, right? Aren't you guys from Mexico? *(No one's quite sure how to respond …)*

EMMA. You know, I'm continually surprised by the quality of the American public school system.

KIM. Tell me about it. In my high school yearbook I was voted "Most Likely To Be A Good Mother." What kind of bullshit is that? I can't even take care of my Sims. You guys know that video game? Well, mine all died. I forgot to send those little fuckers to work and so they had no money to buy food so they starved and died. I cried. I actually cried when my Sims died. Those tiny bastards never had a chance. *(Kim toasts the heavens and shoots her tequila. Myron joins her, then fills her glass with more tequila. Emma and Charlie stare.)*

CHARLIE. One can be an illegal alien from any country.

MYRON. Or planet.

CHARLIE. Or planet, thanks. It just means you are in the country without permission from the government.

KIM. Well, then how come when they talk about it on the news they only show pictures of Mexicans?

EMMA. Well, they do seem to get caught a bit more often than the rest of us.

KIM. Maybe it's 'cause they're brown; easier to spot in a crowd. Racism, I guess.

MYRON. You are so wise.

KIM. I'm going to college on the internet. *(Beat.)* I'm studying feelings.

MYRON. I have those.

KIM. So if you're here illegally, why don't you travel back to your homeland?

EMMA. *(Flustered.)* Well, I … left England …

MYRON. Emma's an American trapped in a Brit's body. This is her home now.

KIM. *(Re: the house.)* It's so nice.

EMMA. No, not this particular home. He meant the nation.

KIM. Oh. Got it. Well ... welcome.

CHARLIE. Yes, welcome. I'm very happy you've all made your-selves at home here, but what do you say we move this whole shindig down to the firehouse, huh? That could be fun. Hey, there's even a pole for *you.*

EMMA. We're not leaving you alone.

MYRON. I'm the one who's gonna have to come back and cut you down if you go through with it, so we might as well stay here and enjoy this stunning view of Manhattan we've acquired.

EMMA. Oh please, Myron, stop fawning; you're embarrassing yourself.

MYRON. Jealousy's a horrible color on you, Emma. It's obvious that Kim and I have a connection.

CHARLIE. I guess I'm just gonna have to go and call the police then.

MYRON. Or I could just call them on my radio and have them take you down to the Ocean County psych ward. That's what we're supposed to do ... *(Myron and Charlie stare each other down.)*

KIM. Why would you wanna be left alone, Charlie? Don't you like company? I'm relatively new at this, but you are the first person to turn down my services. Do you prefer penises?

CHARLIE. No.

KIM. It's okay if you do.

CHARLIE. I'm not gay.

KIM. I'm not dirty. I don't have any STDs or anything. I thought I had crabs once, but it turned out it was just scabies.

CHARLIE. What are scabies?

KIM. They're like these tiny microscopic bugs that crawl under your skin and take tiny microscopic shits. Your skin is allergic to their tiny shits, so you start to itch and get rashes all over.

MYRON. The sun is slowly setting on my view.

EMMA. So you caught this, the microscopic insect shit, you caught this from a customer.

KIM. Yes and no. He wanted to fuck me in a sandbox. Twisted guy. You wouldn't believe how much he paid me to fuck him in a sand-box in a playground up by the 79th Street boat basin. Turns out that's where they like to live. That's why little kids get scabies all the time.

MYRON. Because they fuck in sandboxes?

KIM. No. Because they *play* in sandboxes. And that's where scabies like to live. So I go to the doctor and I'm like, "What's with all these itchy bumps; do I have crabs?" So he tells me to pull down my pants.

MYRON. I shoulda gone to med school.

KIM. He takes a really close look at my pussy … and says —

MYRON. "Turn that frown upside down."

KIM. No, he says, "Don't worry, it's not crabs, it's just scabies."

EMMA. How do you kill scabies?

KIM. There's a lotion. You have to rub it all over your body and clean all your clothes and sheets. But I couldn't help but feel really bad for the guy. I mean, apparently scabies spread like wildfire.

MYRON. As a fireman, I can tell you that wildfires spread very quickly.

CHARLIE. He must have given it to his wife and kids.

EMMA. Well, I'm sure the scabies were happy, they got to hitch a ride on those kids right back to the sandbox.

KIM. Anyway, the point is, Charlie …

CHARLIE. Yes, what was the point?

KIM. The point is that I'm clean. Kevin has been very good to me and helped me out a lot, so I don't want to let him down.

CHARLIE. How exactly has Kevin been good to you? *(The action on stage freezes as the scrim quickly flies in and covers the proscenium of the entire stage. A pre-shot video flickers to life on the scrim. We are in Kevin O'Donnell's very expensive New York loft. Expensive art adorns the walls. Kevin and Kim have just finished fucking.)*

KEVIN. Oh fuck! Fuck!

KIM. Fuck. Stupid condoms.

KEVIN. Oh my God, I just came in a prostitute. Do you have AIDS?! Please tell me you don't have AIDS!

KIM. Okay, calm down! I don't have AIDS.

KEVIN. Well, you're on the pill, right?

KIM. Hell no!

KEVIN. Hell no? How could you say "hell, no"? You're a prostitute! It seems like a relatively important business expenditure for someone who fucks strangers for money.

KIM. I just don't like to put weird chemicals in my body.

KEVIN. You put strangers' cocks inside your body! How could you possibly draw the line at concentrated estrogen?!

KIM. Those pills are so bad for you.

KEVIN. And so is stranger-cock, but you don't seem to have a problem taking that!

KIM. You're not being very nice.

KEVIN. You're just gonna have to take "the morning after pill."

KIM. Maybe.

KEVIN. No. No maybe! I just came inside of you. I cannot get you pregnant! My wife's already pregnant!

KIM. Will you help me pay for my demo?

KEVIN. What?!

KIM. My music demo. Haven't you listened to me all day? I told you I'm trying to get my music career going and I need a little extra cash to pay for a demo.

KEVIN. Oh my God, you're blackmailing me? This is horrible. From orgasm to blackmail in less than thirty seconds; that has to be a record.

KIM. I'm not blackmailing you. I'm just offering up a swap: demo for abortion.

KEVIN. It's not an abortion! How is it an abortion?! I just came ten seconds ago! Nothing's been fertilized!

KIM. Well, that depends on who you ask. Sarah Palin would probably say it's an abortion.

KEVIN. Jesus Christ.

KIM. Just think of it as supporting the arts.

KEVIN. Look around you; I already support the arts. My art dealer just talked me into spending a quarter-million dollars on some bullshit piece of African art. I threw it into my beach house. It's made up of hundreds of these little beads. *(Beat.)* How much is a demo?

KIM. Fifty-thousand will work.

KEVIN. To sing into a microphone?! I'll buy you a fucking karaoke machine.

KIM. No! I need to work with this producer "DJ Cracker Hater." I met him in Atlantic City and he really understands what I'm going for.

KEVIN. If he hates crackers, why does he want to work with you?

KIM. What the hell do I have to do with him not liking crackers? I'm not a fucking Pringle.

KEVIN. "Cracker" is a derogatory name for white people. He hates white people.

KIM. He does not hate white people. That's just his alias. He's Jewish. I know 'cause I fucked him last *Shabbas*. I remember 'cause I had to turn off the lights; he's not allowed to operate a light switch on the Sabbath.

KEVIN. He can fuck a prostitute, but he can't touch a light switch?

KIM. Yeah. God wants him to rest, I guess. Weird, huh? I'm tired too. Where's my fucking *Shabbas*?

KEVIN. Okay. Fine! Whatever. But I wanna watch you eat those pills.

KIM. Oh yay! Kevin, thank you so much! I'm so happy you believe in me! Now I'm glad you shot your load in me; I'm gonna be a star. *(The clip ends. Lights up behind the scrim as it flies out.)* He's been very supportive of my music career. I'm actually a singer/songwriter. I just do this to pay my rent. Kevin's helping to produce my EP.

MYRON. Do you mind if I ask ... and please tell me if this is out of line, but how much does it cost to have the luxury of your services?

CHARLIE. That is is outta line. Don't answer that.

KIM. I'm very expensive. I mean no offense, but regular working guys such as yourself are often shocked at the price. But I'm the top level. I mean, I'm like the Louis Vuitton of vagina.

EMMA. What does that cost? How much did Kevin pay you for the night?

KIM. You're gonna gasp.

EMMA. No, we won't.

CHARLIE. Don't say it. We don't wanna know.

MYRON. Oh, yes we do!

KIM. Promise you won't freak out and drop your jaws?

EMMA. We promise.

CHARLIE. You don't owe anyone here anything.

MYRON. We're not judging you, we're just curious ...

KIM. Fifteen-thousand.

CHARLIE. Are you serious?

KIM. But I'll do anything.

MYRON. Sweetheart, I'll fuck a *bear* for fifteen-thousand dollars. You can take a syringe full of scabies and shoot them into my eyes for fifteen K. Fuck! How fucked up is our society?! These guys like Kevin O'Donnell up there on Wall Street are dumping more money into whores ...

KIM.	CHARLIE.
Hey!	Come on!

MYRON. Sorry. "Escorts" … than I make in six months protecting an entire island from going up in flames. And you know what really kills me? Who bailed them out? Who the fuck bailed them out when they were drowning up to their Bluetooth earpieces in bad loans and debt? Me. The regular working guys you're talking about. They took my money and gave it to the Kevin O'Donnells of the world, so they could fuck whores and produce whore records.

EMMA. Myron!

MYRON. And you know, technically … the thing is … I mean, if you really wanna zoom out; in the macro of this situation, I have personally paid for a fraction of tonight's services. And I would like to redeem my portion now. What do you say, Charlie?

CHARLIE. He paid you fifteen-thousand dollars to sleep with me?

KIM. Yes. But look how cute I am. And I came all the way down here to Long Beach Island. And you can do whatever you want to me …

EMMA. Except for your asshole …

KIM. Yeah, except for my asshole.

MYRON. I have a similar policy.

CHARLIE. Look, it was a nice thing for Kevin to do. He gave me the finest thing he could afford to cheer me up.

EMMA. A fuck? Is that the finest thing a rich man can afford?

CHARLIE. No. He sent me some company. He rented me some friendship.

KIM. Totes. We have this thing called GFE. It stands for "the girlfriend experience." One guy I never even slept with, he just wanted to cuddle. I hugged the guy for a week and made like fifty-thousand dollars.

MYRON. Could I have his number?

KIM. No.

MYRON. I will hug the shit out of that guy. I will literally hug him until he shits the bed from too much hugging.

CHARLIE. God, people will do anything to avoid being alone.

EMMA. You wanna be alone.

CHARLIE. I do now, but not … before. Before I would do anything I could to avoid being alone. I'd scroll through my phone just looking for someone to text. In line for coffee, in the car; I always had to be talking or texting someone …

EMMA. Are you lonely, Charlie?

CHARLIE. Of course I'm lonely.

EMMA. Then why are you trying so hard to get rid of us? Isn't this what you want? You're lonely and here you are surrounded by other people.

KIM. Maybe it's like being bone-tired. You feel bone-lonesome.

CHARLIE. *(A small smile.)* Hmm. That's actually kind of a good way to put it.

EMMA. Is that why you wanna kill yourself?

KIM. Excuse me, what?

MYRON. Oh yeah. We forgot to tell you about that. We all got a little caught up in the excitement of your arrival and the micro-scopic bugs taking shits under your skin. By the way, he also claims he's murdered a bunch of people.

KIM. You're a murderer? Oh my God, we need to make a citizen's arrest.

CHARLIE. Kim, wait. No, you don't.

KIM. Don't worry; I've got handcuffs in my purse.

CHARLIE. Kim. *(While Kim rifles through her purse looking for her handcuffs, she pulls out a large, pink dildo and waves it at Charlie like a weapon.)*

KIM. Don't you come near me!

EMMA. We can't arrest him; Charlie's a hero who's flown hundreds of sorties to Iraq.

KIM. Why would a sorority wanna go to Iraq?

EMMA. Sorties, not sororities. Missions. When I found him earlier he was on that chair with this noose around his neck.

KIM. Oh my God, there's a noose! He's gonna lynch us. We gotta get outta here!

EMMA. Careful! *(Kim races towards the door, but slips violently on the African beads on the floor.)*

KIM. Ow! Fuck!

MYRON. Somebody should really sweep up those beads.

EMMA. Are you okay?

KIM. He's got this place booby-trapped like *Home Alone!*

MYRON. Thank you! *(Myron and Emma race to help her up. She limps on her ankle over to a chair.)*

EMMA. Oh my God. Are you okay? We had an incident with a faulty piece of culture. I'll get you some ice.

KIM. No, it's okay; my drink didn't spill. *(Beat.)* Please don't lynch us! We won't tell anyone you're gay.

CHARLIE. I'm not gay.

KIM. That's exactly what we'll say.

CHARLIE. It was an accident!

MYRON. An accident! Now we're getting somewhere.

KIM. Were you the one who started the fire?

CHARLIE. There was no fire! This guy's a liar; he's probably not even a fireman!

KIM. Wait a minute, I'm confused.

MYRON. Shocking! *(They hear a loud siren out front.)*

KIM. Oh, thank God, the cops.

CHARLIE. *(To Myron)* You called the police?!

MYRON. No, that's our cocaine! Be right back. *(Myron exits through the front door.)*

EMMA. Kim, I think you can relax about Charlie trying to hurt you. The noose is for him.

KIM. What?! Why would you want to hang yourself on your birthday?

EMMA. Is it your birthday, Charlie?

CHARLIE. Yes.

EMMA. How old are you?

CHARLIE. Thirty-five.

EMMA. Happy birthday! Drinks all around! *(Emma crosses to the bar to grab the whiskey. She fills both of their glasses.)*

KIM. But isn't he a murderer?

EMMA. We haven't exactly gotten the details yet. Myron says he's lying. Myron thinks Charlie's made up the whole story to impress me.

KIM. That's so romantic. I hope you're lying; it's your birthday. You should be celebrating.

EMMA. That's a great idea. We should throw you a party.

CHARLIE. Please don't.

EMMA. Look, if you've really got your heart set on doing it tonight, then do it later when we've all left. You might as well spend your last night alive celebrating the day you were born.

CHARLIE. That makes absolutely no sense.

KIM. Why not?

CHARLIE. Why would I wanna celebrate the day I was born? If I'm really gonna kill myself, wouldn't it make more sense to celebrate the day I finally get to die? *(Myron opens the door holding a bag of coke in one hand and a snowball in the other.)*

26

MYRON. I've got New Jersey snow and Colombian snow. Which one do you want to bring in the house?

KIM. Colombian! Colombian!

MYRON. Colombian it is! *(Myron tosses the snowball outside.)*

KIM. Oh, thank God!

EMMA. Myron, it's Charlie's birthday.

MYRON. Killing yourself on your birthday? That's morbid. Now who wants some Cheetos and some nitrous oxide?

EMMA. Oooh, I'll have some nitrous. It'll help me add a whole other dimension to Charlie's party. Please tell me you remembered the balloons. *(Myron produces two empty balloons.)* There they are! We need a theme. And I'm choosing birthday, Charlie: It's far less twisted and weird. I'm guessing you don't believe in the afterlife?

CHARLIE. No, just purgatory.

EMMA. That's it, then ... soul shuts off like a light switch?

CHARLIE. That would be the goal.

EMMA. Well, we might be able to get away with a death-day party if you believed in the afterlife. I mean if you had like seventy-two virgins waiting for you on the other side and all that, maybe we'd have something to toast ... *(Myron begins to cut up lines of coke on the coffee table. Kim kneels next to him, eager for a turn.)*

KIM. Who gets seventy-two virgins?

MYRON. Some Muslims believe that if you die as a martyr, you get to have seventy-two virgins as a "thank you" present when you get to heaven.

KIM. I mean, I guess that's nice and all. But virgins aren't very experienced are they? I'd much rather have like twenty ridiculously good lovers as my present. Or I guess if they were Latin I'd probably only need ten. *(Kim does a line of coke.)*

CHARLIE. Are you planning on dying as a martyr?

KIM. Maybe.

CHARLIE. *(Sarcastically.)* Okay.

KIM. What's a martyr?

MYRON. A martyr is someone who dies for their religious beliefs.

KIM. Oh, then never mind. I'm Catholic; I don't think we get virgins. But if we do, I'd really like to know ahead of time. I hate surprises. It's like when I'm on the phone with a client; I always like to know going in what he wants. That way I have the upper hand when he tries to surprise me with something like asking me to piss on him.

EMMA. People pay you to piss on them?

KIM. All the time. A lot of politicians actually; it's like their thing. If I just piss on them while they beat off, they don't feel like they cheated on their wives and then they won't really be lying to voters when they say they love family values and all the other values that those guys have to make sure they love.

EMMA. God, people are so twisted, aren't they?

KIM. What do you mean?

EMMA. Sweetheart, if someone's got the money … they can own you and do whatever they want to you. And I'm sorry, but that just makes me very sad. In fact, the only thing that makes me sadder than that … is how busy you probably are …

KIM. Jeez, you make it sound so horrible. I think some people are just kinky fucks who ended up in a society where they're not allowed to be as twisted as they want to be. So they hold down all the things they lust for as much as they can, but sometimes it's just too hard. Did you ever see that movie *The Ten Commandments* with the guy who loves guns as Moses?

MYRON. Charlton Heston.

KIM. Right. Well, we had to watch that movie every Easter at my house. And when the guy who loves guns goes up to get the Ten Commandments, there's like this major fun party going on at the bottom of Mount Sinus. People are drinking and screwing and dancing. It's like a fucking rave. To me as a kid, it always looked like so much fun. Maybe God didn't fully understand what He created. I know with my Sims, for example, they got super into playing darts. I had nothing to do with that; I fucking hate darts. But I created them and then they got into their own thing. Maybe we're really supposed to be free and crazy and sometimes a little twisted. Charlton Moses shouldn't have got so mad just 'cause they wanted to party.

CHARLIE. He was mad that they were worshiping an idol.

KIM. What?

CHARLIE. Charlton Moses! *(Beat.)* The party you didn't want to end was to worship the statue of a cow. Moses comes down from the mountain, and he gets so pissed that they're all worshiping this cow statue, that he drops the commandments and kills the 3,000 people at your party. It's kind of a funny story actually. I mean, the poor guy's exhausted; he's been sleeping on the side of a cliff for forty days and he's all ready to tell everybody, "Hey guys, this just in; thou shall not kill." But he gets so pissed off about the worshiping of the cow idol that he brutally slaughters 3,000 people in the name of God.

KIM. Buzzkill.

EMMA. Bible scholar?

CHARLIE. Hebrew school. Most of the kids stuck to the coloring book version; I actually read the damn thing. God has a temper.

EMMA. For someone who doesn't particularly like God, you certainly know a lot about Him.

CHARLIE. God, the character in the book, is vengeful and angry.

EMMA. Do you ever talk to God, Charlie? *(Beat.)*

CHARLIE. I'm tired of this. I'm going upstairs.

MYRON. No, you're not. We're not letting you out of our sight. We've been good to you. We've kept you outta the padded room. I think you owe us an explanation.

CHARLIE. I don't owe you anything! I don't even know who the fuck you people are! As far as I can tell, you're just a sad bunch of drug addicts who refuse to leave me alone!

MYRON. What kind of people would we be if we let you kill yourself?! And don't you think it's odd that you chose one of the most desolate places on the Eastern seaboard to end your life and within seconds of you standing on that chair, there was someone knocking on the door to stop you?

CHARLIE. It was a coincidence; not divine intervention!

MYRON. And then me and then Kim. Open your fucking eyes, man! We're here! *(The action on stage freezes as the scrim flies in and covers the entire proscenium. A pre-shot video is projected on the front of the scrim. Myron sits across the desk from Ramona, a school principal.)*

RAMONA. I got a call this morning, Myron, from an angry parent. Not unusual. In my position, someone's always upset. What I'm not used to, is this particular complaint. Do you have a Facebook account, Myron?

MYRON. I do. *(Beat.)* I use it to keep track of all my kids. I think it's very useful to see what they're all up to? Keep an eye on them, if you will.

RAMONA. Uh-huh. And did you use this … social networking … device to contact some of your students; to ask them about a cast party?

MYRON. Hmmm. You know, I don't really recall.

RAMONA. Well, let me help you jog your memory. Did you attend a cast party at Ryan Freedman's house in which over sixty-five of our students were drinking and consuming narcotics?

MYRON. Ryan Freedman. He's the adopted Filipino kid who plays the mascot?

RAMONA. Yes, Ryan plays "Scalpy the Native American" for the football team.

MYRON. I thought the school board was gonna change his name to something more P.C. than "Scalpy the Indian."

RAMONA. Don't change the subject, Myron; you know very well I fielded all those complaints and negotiated with the alumni and that's why we've renamed him "Scalpy the *Native American.*"

MYRON. Yes, but he's still a scalper. I mean, he's still running around the field with a plastic sickle trying to scalp the other teams' mascots …

RAMONA. Myron. Are these not pictures on Facebook of you doing drugs with members of the student body? *(Myron looks at Ramona's computer screen. We see a close-up of a photo of him snorting lines with a student in a "Scalpy" mascot costume.)*

MYRON. I'm not gonna lie. That guy does look a lot like me; a really fucked-up version of me. But I have a common look. No one's ever told me I look like the same celebrity. I get everything from Iggy Pop to Morgan Freeman. Are there any other angles? *(She clicks through multiple pictures of him doing drugs with students.)*

RAMONA. You're on fucking Facebook snorting cocaine with your students! Are you out of your mind?! Are you an insane person? *(Myron thinks.)*

MYRON. They're happy. It's nice to be around them. Everyone my age is so miserable. I mean, have you ever sat in the teachers' lounge? A conversation about anything instantaneously devolves into complaining about everything. *(Beat.)* When I was in college, people used to cheer when I walked into the room. We belly-laughed. We were silly. I miss that. These kids are my friends. *(Beat.)* What a shame.

RAMONA. You should have bought a cat. You're fired. *(Lights up behind the scrim as it quickly flies out.)*

EMMA. Okay, everybody take a deep breath. Myron, you taught drama for ten years. Can't you put on some type of show or something? Provide some bloody entertainment for Charlie's party.

KIM. Dance like Usher!

MYRON. I'm not a fucking court jester. I'm a public servant. I need to retain my dignity. *(Myron snorts a line of coke.)*

EMMA. But it might be nice for Charlie's birthday if you could quote something beautiful; something that might remind him of the sanctity of life, et cetera.

MYRON. "The sanctity of life, et cetera?" Let me see what I have stored on that subject …

CHARLIE. That's okay. I'm alright.

MYRON. What's your pleasure, birthday boy? Molière, Stoppard, Pinter?

CHARLIE. Please don't do me any favors.

MYRON. It would be my honor to perform for the king of the castle. What is your pleasure, good sir?

KIM. Come on, Charlie.

EMMA. Come on, don't be shy.

CHARLIE. *(Beat.)* I don't know! I don't know things like that. In high school we put on a production of *The Merchant of Venice.*

MYRON. Elizabethan anti-Semitism; that's light and fun. Who did you play?

CHARLIE. I didn't. I was on the lighting crew. My job was to keep a spotlight focused on this handicapped kid that was playing … what's the main character's name? Sherlock?

MYRON. Yes, Sherlock, part-time money-lender, part-time Jewish detective. Shylock.

CHARLIE. Shylock. Whatever. *(Beat.)* I do remember being very moved by the courage of this kid rolling around the stage in his electric wheelchair saying this poetry about how he was human too. I mean, I know the lines are about a Jewish guy and everything, but night after night, I followed him with this spotlight as he rolled around the stage, and, I swear, I got tears in my eyes every single time. For him it was about being this totally normal kid who was like … trapped in this costume of a freak; and he was using the poetry to scream out to all the other kids like, "I'm human too … I'm in here … can anybody fucking hear me?" You know? *(Beat.)* And I heard him. *(Beat.)*

EMMA. Give us a little Shylock, Myron. It's his birthday. Show us what you've got.

MYRON. It's been a very long time.

EMMA. Just a li'l sampler … A little Shylock sampler platter …

KIM. Yes, please! For Charlie … I'll make it worth your while!

MYRON. Elaborate, my dear.

KIM. You can feel my tits.

MYRON. Under the bra.

KIM. Bra? What is this, a wedding?

31

MYRON. Done and done. Here, Charlie; focus your spotlight on this … *(He hands Charlie a flashlight from his belt. Emma dims the lights. Charlie shines the light on Myron, casting a giant distorted shadow of him on the back wall. He does the following quite well.)* "Hath not a Jew eyes? Hath not a Jew hands, organs, dimensions, senses, affections, passions; fed with the same food, hurt with the same weapons, subject to the same diseases, healed by the same means, warmed and cooled by the same winter and summer as a Christian is? If you prick us, do we not bleed? If you tickle us, do we not laugh? If you poison us, do we not die? And if you wrong us, shall we not revenge?" *(He takes a bow as the three of them applaud. Emma returns the lights to normal.)*

EMMA. Bravo.

KIM. That was so beautiful.

MYRON. I still got it. Not much demand for Billy Shakes down at the firehouse. My prize?

EMMA. You don't have to let him …

KIM. It's okay, Emma, I'm a woman of my word. Just don't go crazy. *(Kim stands in front of Myron. Myron puts his hands up her shirt and grabs her breasts.)*

MYRON. Dear God.

KIM. Your hands are cold.

MYRON. Sweetheart, shhh; I'm on the phone with God. So this is what perfect breasts feel like. I've always wondered.

KIM. They're real too.

MYRON. Of course they are. Hello, new friends.

KIM. Hey, Emma; I was thinking.

MYRON. Wait, don't think just yet. *(As if composing a letter.)* Dear Jesus …

KIM. Okay, that's weird. *(She removes his hands.)*

MYRON. I'll never wash my hands again.

EMMA. Oh, wonderful, scabies for everyone!

KIM. I was thinking; we could do a whole talent show for Charlie's birthday. Everyone'll do what they're good at; I can sing you one of my songs …

EMMA. And I'll smoke weed and eat lots of pills. It's a wonderful idea. This is gonna be perfect. We need to make it more festive, though. I'm gonna take this box of nitrous and search around the house and see if I can find some decorations and presents.

KIM. I can help! I love snooping through my clients' houses when they're asleep. That's how I got this Rolex.

EMMA. You must have some wonderful stories, Kim ...

KIM. Well, I once got to beat off Ozzy Osbourne.

EMMA. Wow.

KIM. Yeah; he came dust. *(Emma and Kim climb the stairs. Myron lights a cigarette. They stand there awkwardly for a long beat.)*

CHARLIE. You taught high school drama for ten years?

MYRON. Yes.

CHARLIE. I guess that's why you're so smart, huh?

MYRON. I prefer clever.

CHARLIE. You've always got some obnoxious quip just ... ready to go, huh?

MYRON. You know those people who just enjoy fucking with people?

CHARLIE. Yes.

MYRON. I'm one of those people.

CHARLIE. I can tell.

MYRON. Why did you make up that story about being a fighter pilot?

CHARLIE. What are you talking about?

MYRON. Why are you exerting so much energy lying to us about who you are and what you've done?

CHARLIE. Why are you so positive I'm lying?

MYRON. You said you flew the F-22 Raptor ...

CHARLIE. Yes.

MYRON. In Iraq and Afghanistan?

CHARLIE. Yes.

MYRON. The Military Channel just did a story about how they aren't using the F-22 Raptor in the Middle East. The technology is so advanced and top-secret, that the chance of one being downed behind enemy lines isn't worth the risk. So even though it's the most advanced war machine man has ever made, and cost one hundred million dollars each to produce, it isn't fighting in either of our two wars. There's a few hundred of them sitting on a tarmac somewhere, just waiting for China to ask for their loans back. *(Beat.)* You just phoned in a bad lie ... *(Beat.)* Why?

CHARLIE. What does it matter?

MYRON. I'm just curious.

CHARLIE. I mean, isn't it obvious? I wanted to seem a bit more than I am ...

33

MYRON. Yes, but why? Why would a suicidal man care so much about what people thought of him? Why do you care? You're gonna be dead. It's like a drowning man wanting the lifeguards to know he's a good swimmer. *(The sound of laughter as Emma and Kim cross from one side of the upstairs bridge to the other. Kim picks up a small statue of a man.)*

KIM. This little man should come with us! *(She carries it out. Myron waits until they are gone.)*

MYRON. Did you leave a note?

CHARLIE. No.

MYRON. Why not? Don't the people that love you deserve an explanation? Although, I'll bet it's the rare occasion where someone reads a suicide note and says, "Fuck. You know, I was skeptical when I started this thing, but I have to say, he made the right call on this one. His life was pretty fucked."

CHARLIE. It's a long story. I didn't think it would fit in a note.

MYRON. I mean, I can understand that you're depressed maybe, but not why you wanna off yourself. And why hanging? If I ever killed myself, it would be in a much more civil manner: the car-in-the-garage thing. Put on a little Steely Dan and fall right to sleep. Hanging is so … violent.

CHARLIE. That's good to know. Next time I'll make sure to do it in a way that's less upsetting to you.

MYRON. Just gimme a little something. Gimme a piece of the truth and I'll leave you alone. *(Charlie is silent for a beat. He looks at the record player downstage.)*

CHARLIE. You know this, like, Irish … like *Riverdance* music? *(He leans down and puts the record on for a few seconds. The song from the top of the show plays through the record player's speaker. He stops it.)*

CHARLIE. I fucking hate that music. *(Myron smiles.)* And I was dating this girl. And she just loved it. She would always dance around the house to it in her underwear doing all these made-up little "jigs." And it was so funny 'cause she knew I hated it, but she loved how she could always make me laugh with her funny little made-up dance moves. *(Beat.)* She was so beautiful and sweet and put up with me being … a little less than fun. But she wanted to do stuff and travel and you know … see the world like young, pretty girls do … and should. And I … couldn't do that. So … she hung in there as long as she could, but … eventually, she had enough. And the last time I ever saw her she handed me that record of Irish

34

folk music. *(He smiles.)*

MYRON. And you're not a fighter pilot.

CHARLIE. No. I'm not. That just sounded so exciting.

MYRON. What are you then? Lemme guess: a motivational speaker.

CHARLIE. I'm an air-traffic controller. I *was* an air-traffic controller. *(The scrim flies in. The pre-shot video is projected on the scrim. We see a close-up of the radar screen. The camera reveals Charlie looking off, distracted. We hear the sound effects of an air-traffic controller office. As real-life Charlie speaks, he crosses in front of the scrim. The imagery in the film is projected on top of him and the scrim. Myron is picked out the whole time with a light special behind [or beside] the scrim.)* Normally, I handled the busiest section of the approach into Newark, JFK and LaGuardia. I mean, this is like the craziest airspace in the entire world. But my supervisor knew I hadn't been myself for a while, so he'd put me on a sector further south in the middle of the state that was less busy. And one day, as I'm staring off into space, I got distracted by these two ants on my console. *(We see a close-up of the two ants.)* They were fighting over a tiny crumb from the Pop-Tart I had eaten for breakfast. It was the strangest thing. It was like I went into a trance. All I could see were these two little insects, fighting over something that was so important to them; so crucial to their survival. But they couldn't see it from my perspective. *I* could see with such clarity that that Pop-Tart crumb meant absolutely nothing. And then I thought, well, if there is a God, that's probably how He feels when He looks down at me. He's probably cracking himself up watching me wrestle myself over nothing. And so for the first time in my whole life, I felt this odd connection to God. And so I thought I should pray. So I closed my eyes and I prayed. I prayed for Him to help me see how I was being just as ridiculous as those two stupid ants. *(Charlie walks in front of the imagery, it's projected on his face and body.)* "God? I'm here. And I need your help. And I know I'm not starving, I know I'm not fighting in some war, I'm not sick, but I am stuck in this pit. Can you pull me out? Can you help me? Can you save me with a sign?"

PILOT 1. *(On radio.)* New York Approach, Gulfstream 34 Apple-Delta, we're getting a traffic warning, but we're in complete IMC, please advise about traffic at our two o'clock!

PILOT 2. *(On radio.)* New York Approach, this is Cirrus Pappa-Delta-One, we've got the same warning at our seven! Is it an error? He's at our altitude; it looks like this guy's headed right for us! *(A supervisor comes over.)*

SUPERVISOR. Holy shit. 34 Apple-Delta, turn to heading 270! Cirrus, climb at best rate now! Charlie, what the fuck are you doing?! *(The imagery of the two planes on the radar screen hit and then disappear. Screaming and mayhem on the radio echoes! Lights up behind scrim as it flies out.)*

MYRON. *(Putting it all together.)* The six people. I remember it on the news.

CHARLIE. Five died on impact. One of the planes actually had a parachute that deployed. So the mother of this family lived through the night. *(Beat.)* The inquiry ruled it an accident. They suspended me for one hundred days. One hundred days! It works out to 16.6 days per life. I don't think that's enough …

MYRON. So you sentenced yourself to death …

CHARLIE. So I sentenced myself to death.

MYRON. *(Beat.)* Whatever happened to those ants?

CHARLIE. The ants? I hadn't seen them. *(A slight smile.)* The ants gave up and left that crumb behind. I actually kept it in my wallet. Wanna see it?

MYRON. Sure … *(Charlie pulls a tiny piece of folded tinfoil out of his wallet and unfolds it on the coffee table, revealing a tiny crumb. He and Myron sit there staring at it. Emma and Kim reenter from upstairs. Emma has Christmas lights and a giant red exercise ball. Kim has a ukulele.)*

EMMA. Well, we didn't find much in terms of decorations, but I found these Christmas lights and this exercise ball. Here, Charlie, this is from all of us. *(She throws the big ball to Charlie. He catches it.)*

KIM. Charlie, I've got good news: I found this ukulele. I'm gonna play you a song. *(She notices Myron staring at the crumb.)* What are you looking at?

MYRON. A Pop-Tart crumb.

KIM. I love Pop-Tarts.

EMMA. Are you that hungry? Order a fucking pizza.

MYRON. Don't eat it, it's a memento of Charlie's. *(Charlie and Myron look in each other's eyes.)*

EMMA. Myron, help me string these up. *(He doesn't move.)* Myron? Snap out of it. Help me string these around a little. *(He helps her string the lights around the room. Kim cuts a line of coke on the table next to the Pop-Tart crumb.)*

KIM. I'm so excited I found this ukulele, 'cause now I can play you a song. I have to decide if I'm gonna play you one of mine, or one of somebody else's. I mean, most of mine are sad little love songs. But you guys seem more like an indie-rock, Williamsburg kinda crowd ... *(She snorts a line of coke.)* Oh fuck!

EMMA. What?

KIM. Fuck! Fuck! Fuck!

EMMA. What?

KIM. Charlie, I'm so sorry, but I think I may have just accidentally snorted your special Pop-Tart crumb.

MYRON. Are you fucking kidding me?!

KIM. It was an accident, I was talking and snorting at the same time and I wasn't paying attention. Don't worry, I can vomit it up. *(She sticks her fingers down her throat. And begins to gag.)*

ALL THREE. No!

KIM. Relax! I do it all the time.

MYRON. What is wrong with you?

KIM. I'm sorry, I got distracted.

MYRON. And anyway stay away from my coke; you're like a fucking Dustbuster.

KIM. I feel awful. It was important to him. If someone snorted my hamster, Chanel, I'd be so pissed!

MYRON. You're a fucking idiot.

EMMA. Myron, relax. It's a crumb.

MYRON. You don't know the full context, Emma.

EMMA. Lemme go out on a limb here: The full context was the full Pop-Tart? *(Charlie laughs. They all stare at him.)*

MYRON. What the hell are *you* laughing at?

CHARLIE. *(Smiling.)* She's right. *(Beat.)* It was just a crumb, right? *(To Kim.)* It was just a crumb. Don't worry about it. *(Beat.)* It's yours now. *(Kim starts to tune the ukulele. Her tuning of the uke scores the next section of the play. Myron sits solemnly in the corner. Emma lights a joint and sits down next to Charlie.)*

EMMA. It's nice to see you laugh, Charlie. My dad could always make me laugh like that with his jokes. I haven't been able to talk to him for a while. I miss him quite a bit.

CHARLIE. I know a joke.

EMMA. You do? Well, let's have it.

CHARLIE. God, I haven't told a joke in a long time.

EMMA. Well, go for it. No judgments ...

CHARLIE. *(He sits down next to her and takes a hit of the joint.)*

What's the last thing you wanna hear right after you have sex with Willie Nelson?

EMMA. What?

CHARLIE. *(Tiny beat.)* "I'm not Willie Nelson." *(Emma laughs. Charlie smiles. They share the joint. Myron looks on possessively.)*

EMMA. You know, you really are cute. When I first saw you hanging there, I didn't notice. But you really are. If you don't go through with it, maybe we could go out sometime. And then, one day, we'll fall in love and have a zillion little babies together. And every single one of them will have big, beautiful, blue … passports. That's what we all want, isn't it?

CHARLIE. Passports?

EMMA. No. Someone to love. Someone to wrap their arms around us and just make us feel … unique. Like it somehow matters that we're here, you know? Love is such a fleeting thing to pin all of our happiness on, isn't it? It's like trying to build a house of cards on the back of a squirrel.

MYRON. You've got a lot of nerve, Emma.

EMMA. Excuse me?

MYRON. Doing this right in front of me when you know how I feel about you?

EMMA. Oh, please, don't start this now. We're all having such a good time at Charlie's party.

MYRON. You know what, just be honest with me for once and for all: Why am I not worthy of your love?

EMMA. You are worthy of my friendship, Myron. I enjoy you. I appreciate you. But for the last time, I cannot love you.

MYRON. Do you think I'm ugly?

EMMA. No, not at all.

MYRON. I make you laugh, I loan you money, I …

EMMA. There's no recipe for love. You don't just go "this plus this plus this equals love"; it doesn't work like that. It's either there or it's not. Is that the only reason you're nice to me? To win me over?

MYRON. I'm nice to you because I am completely in love with you. And I might just be the only person who will ever love you. You're damaged goods. *(The room falls silent as Emma gathers her anger and embarrassment. She crosses to Myron.)*

EMMA. Maybe you're right, maybe you are the only person in the world who will ever love me. That would be sad, but maybe that's just what I've been dealt. But I do not love you. And I will not. So you need to let it go. So for the last time: Move on! *(Beat. Suddenly chipper to disguise the emotion.)* Now, I think we should all go around the room and each say something nice about Charlie on his special day. I'll go first. Raise your glasses. *(Myron stays in the kitchen doing coke.)* To Charlie, what can I say? As long as I've known you, you've had your ups and you've had your downs. I can tell you that this night has become a hell of a lot more fun than it ever would have been if it was just another night of me and old Myron drinking down at the firehouse. So I guess what I'm trying to say is, I'm so glad you came down here to Long Beach Island to kill yourself so that I could stop you long enough to tell you that you seem like a very lovely boy. And I can sense that you're very kind ... even though you may or may not have killed some people ... I mean, we all have our faults. I, for instance, am a sucker for chocolate. Anyway, that's it. Happy birthday. Kim?

KIM. Well, when I first saw you, I was really looking forward to fucking you because a lot of the guys that I have to sleep with look like Larry King. But you're really cute. Plus I love soldiers, let alone a fighter pilot, that would be so hot to sleep with you and pretend I'm an Iraqi farmer and you got shot down behind enemy lines and I take you to like my barn or whatever and blow you till you're strong enough to fly us both away to one of those islands with the over-water huts. Anyway ... coke makes me horny, so I hope you change your mind. Amen.

CHARLIE. Amen.

EMMA. Myron? *(Myron does another line of coke.)* Myron, stop sulking. You're being a big baby. Come on! A toast.

MYRON. To Charlie ... the first fighter pilot I've ever met. You're a brave soul, my friend. May you live long enough to realize that you matter. May your neck remain untangled, your feet gravity-bound to our imperfect planet long enough to discover that you are not alone. For even in your lonesome existence, there is love, there is compassion, there is a genuine desire on behalf of these kind strangers to see you discover something that makes your life worth living, Charlie.

EMMA. That was so beautiful.

KIM. Wow, that was pretty.

CHARLIE. Thank you very much.

EMMA. Cheers. *(Myron drinks his full drink.)*

MYRON. Now ... I think we should all go around the room and tell Charlie about the darkest moment in our own lives, so he won't feel so alone in his sadness. Emma, why don't you go first? Why don't you tell Charlie the real reason you can't go back to London? *(Emma stares daggers at Myron.)*

CHARLIE. What are you doing?

MYRON. I just think you might benefit from her story.

EMMA. How dare you? Are you that fucked up? Are you really that fucking pissed that you're gonna break my trust in you?

MYRON. We've all got our skeletons ... Clementine. I just think if you really wanna help Charlie as much as you've fucking advertised, you might consider sharing some of your own pain.

CHARLIE. I really don't want to know.

EMMA. You're doing this because I won't marry you. You know how badly I need to stay in this country, but even that's not enough to feign a marriage to you; because you're disgusting.

MYRON. We don't have anything but an exercise ball to give you for your birthday, Charlie. So I thought we might give you the gift of knowing that you're not alone. Emma claims to wanna save your life. Well, if she really wants to help you, I think she should share a piece of *her* life. Something that happened to *her* ...

CHARLIE. I don't need anything for my birthday.

EMMA. I am not a fucking exhibit! You know, you really are a fucking asshole, Myron. You really are. You're a selfish, self-serving alcoholic! How about that? Why don't you tell Charlie some of your secrets? Give him *that* present. Maybe you could tell him the real reason you were fired from that high school? Why don't you be his friend and share *your* miserable fucking life?

MYRON. Okay, I'll go first. Charlie, I was fired from being a teacher for doing drugs with my kids at a high school cast party. Emma, your turn.

EMMA. I don't want a turn.

CHARLIE. Why are you doing this? Don't do it for me.

MYRON. Well, if you're not gonna tell them, I guess I'll have to ...

KIM. Myron, back the fuck off!

EMMA. Why are you doing this to me?

MYRON. For Charlie; it's his present ...

CHARLIE. I don't want a present, Myron.

MYRON. Charlie, Emma left England ...

EMMA. You gave me your word. You swore on your life.

MYRON. Emma left England because …

CHARLIE. Stop it! Don't say another fucking word.

MYRON. Emma left England …

EMMA. Fine, I'll say it. I left because I was raped. Okay. I was raped by a piece of shit like you.

KIM. Just leave her the fuck alone!

MYRON. But that's not the whole story, is it, Emma?

EMMA. Myron, I'm begging you. I'll love you, I'm sorry, I promise I'll love you.

MYRON. Her rapist was about to get out for good behavior. So jolly old Emma had him killed. They found him in the prison yard with a sharpened toothbrush handle in his heart. Emma's not an American trapped in a Brit's body, she's a Brit trapped in America. *(Beat.)* Ta-da! We all have pain, Charlie. And no one is killing themselves today or ever again. *(Myron violently pulls down the noose from where it is attached to the ceiling. Charlie rushes over to stop him. The cord brings down a chunk of ceiling with it, leaving a small hole in the roof. For a moment they all stare at it as the dust settles.)*

KIM. Oh, my God. You put a hole in the roof. Kevin's gonna be sooooo pissed.

MYRON. *(He crosses through the rubble to push a button on a remote on the fireplace mantel that sparks an instant fire in the fireplace.)* You know, all my favorite movies end with a twist, Charlie. Maybe your twist is that you found something to live for on your thirty-fifth birthday: Moments before you were about to kill yourself, you found some company. Wouldn't *that* be a twist? *(Myron exits.)*

CHARLIE. Everything's gonna be okay.

EMMA. Is it? *(Beat.)* "America the Beautiful" … Amber waves of grain and all that. God shed His grace on thee … When is God gonna shed His grace on *me*, Charlie? When's *that* gonna happen? Because it's been a really long time since anyone's told me that everything was gonna be okay and I was able to believe them.

CHARLIE. What if it's just for tonight? *(Beat. Charlie crosses to her. She looks up at him.)* What if we say just for tonight … everything is gonna be okay? *(A few beats of silence.)*

KIM. You know, I used to work at this phone sex place. And there was this awesome old black woman who went by the name Sensation. She was amazing; she could keep those horny bastards on the phone longer than any of us. Anyway, one day I was crying in one of the bathroom stalls about something and I'm in a super bad mood and feeling sorry for myself and all of a sudden, Sensation opens the door to the stall and she says, "Hey, Princess … " I went by Princess back then. "Hey, Princess," she says, "in a hundred years, there'll be all new people." And I swear I think about that almost every day. *(Beat.)* I never got to give you my present, birthday boy. It was my turn, but the roof fell in. I'm gonna play you one of my songs. It's one of my new ones. *(Kim sits on the couch with her ukulele. Myron watches through the windows as he smokes on the front porch.)*

    WHEN THERE'S NOTHING I CAN SAY TO MAKE
        THINGS BETTER
    I SLING MY ARM AROUND YOUR SHOULDER LIKE
        A SWEATER
    TRY TO BEAR SOME OF THE BURDEN THAT
        YOU'RE WEARING
    BUT I CAN'T SEEM TO LIFT YOU

(A light snow begins to fall outside.)

    WE'LL RALLY, RALLY
    WE'LL RALLY AROUND YOU
    WE'LL RALLY, RALLY AROUND YOU

(A very light snow begins to fall through the hole in the roof that Myron created when he ripped down the noose. Myron stares at them through the window.)

It's snowing. It's snowing in the house.

CHARLIE. You know, I didn't write a suicide note. I didn't write one because I had no one to write it to.

EMMA. It's nice, isn't it, Charlie … it's nice to be with friends on your birthday. *(Beat. They stare into each other's eyes. Charlie smiles. Blackout. The song "The Buzzards of Bourbon Street" by Gaelic Storm [or something like it] returns at full volume. *)*

End of Play

---

* See Special Note on Songs and Recordings on copyright page.

PROPERTY LIST

Cigarettes, lighter
Cell phone
Purse with liquor bottle
Artwork made of beads
Bar with bottles, glasses
Cell phone
Bottle of pills
Bag of cocaine
Snowball
Small statue
Wallet with small square of tinfoil
Christmas lights
Large red exercise ball
Ukulele
Joint
Snow

SOUND EFFECTS

Car alarm
Cell phone rings
Doorbell rings
Siren

NEW PLAYS

★ **YELLOW FACE by David Henry Hwang.** Asian-American playwright DHH leads a protest against the casting of Jonathan Pryce as the Eurasian pimp in the original Broadway production of *Miss Saigon*, condemning the practice as "yellowface." The lines between truth and fiction blur with hilarious and moving results in this unreliable memoir. "A pungent play of ideas with a big heart." –*Variety.* "Fabulously inventive." –*The New Yorker.* [5M, 2W] ISBN: 978-0-8222-2301-6

★ **33 VARIATIONS by Moisés Kaufmann.** A mother coming to terms with her daughter. A composer coming to terms with his genius. And, even though they're separated by 200 years, these two people share an obsession that might, even just for a moment, make time stand still. "A compellingly original and thoroughly watchable play for today." –*Talkin' Broadway.* [4M, 4W] ISBN: 978-0-8222-2392-4

★ **BOOM by Peter Sinn Nachtrieb.** A grad student's online personal ad lures a mysterious journalism student to his subterranean research lab. But when a major catastrophic event strikes the planet, their date takes on evolutionary significance and the fate of humanity hangs in the balance. "Darkly funny dialogue." –*NY Times.* "Literate, coarse, thoughtful, sweet, scabrously inappropriate." –*Washington City Paper.* [1M, 2W] ISBN: 978-0-8222-2370-2

★ **LOVE, LOSS AND WHAT I WORE by Nora Ephron and Delia Ephron, based on the book by Ilene Beckerman.** A play of monologues and ensemble pieces about women, clothes and memory covering all the important subjects—mothers, prom dresses, mothers, buying bras, mothers, hating purses and why we only wear black. "Funny, compelling." –*NY Times.* "So funny and so powerful." –*WowOwow.com.* [5W] ISBN: 978-0-8222-2355-9

★ **CIRCLE MIRROR TRANSFORMATION by Annie Baker.** When four lost New Englanders enrolled in Marty's community center drama class experiment with harmless games, hearts are quietly torn apart, and tiny wars of epic proportions are waged and won. "Absorbing, unblinking and sharply funny." –*NY Times.* [2M, 3W] ISBN: 978-0-8222-2445-7

★ **BROKE-OLOGY by Nathan Louis Jackson.** The King family has weathered the hardships of life and survived with their love for each other intact. But when two brothers are called home to take care of their father, they find themselves strangely at odds. "Engaging dialogue." –*TheaterMania.com.* "Assured, bighearted." –*Time Out.* [3M, 1W] ISBN: 978-0-8222-2428-0

DRAMATISTS PLAY SERVICE, INC.
440 Park Avenue South, New York, NY 10016 212-683-8960 Fax 212-213-1539
postmaster@dramatists.com www.dramatists.com

NEW PLAYS

★ **A CIVIL WAR CHRISTMAS: AN AMERICAN MUSICAL CELEBRA-TION by Paula Vogel, music by Daryl Waters.** It's 1864, and Washington, D.C. is settling down to the coldest Christmas Eve in years. Intertwining many lives, this musical shows us that the gladness of one's heart is the best gift of all. "Boldly inventive theater, warm and affecting." –*Talkin' Broadway.* "Crisp strokes of dialogue." –*NY Times.* [12M, 5W] ISBN: 978-0-8222-2361-0

★ **SPEECH & DEBATE by Stephen Karam.** Three teenage misfits in Salem, Oregon discover they are linked by a sex scandal that's rocked their town. "Savvy comedy." –*Variety.* "Hilarious, cliché-free, and immensely entertaining." –*NY Times.* "A strong, rangy play." –*NY Newsday.* [2M, 2W] ISBN: 978-0-8222-2286-6

★ **DIVIDING THE ESTATE by Horton Foote.** Matriarch Stella Gordon is determined not to divide her 100-year-old Texas estate, despite her family's declining wealth and the looming financial crisis. But her three children have another plan. "Goes for laughs and succeeds." –*NY Daily News.* "The theatrical equivalent of a page-turner." –*Bloomberg.com.* [4M, 9W] ISBN: 978-0-8222-2398-6

★ **WHY TORTURE IS WRONG, AND THE PEOPLE WHO LOVE THEM by Christopher Durang.** Christopher Durang turns political humor upside down with this raucous and provocative satire about America's growing homeland "insecurity." "A smashing new play." –*NY Observer.* "You may laugh yourself silly." –*Bloomberg News.* [4M, 3W] ISBN: 978-0-8222-2401-3

★ **FIFTY WORDS by Michael Weller.** While their nine-year-old son is away for the night on his first sleepover, Adam and Jan have an evening alone together, beginning a suspenseful nightlong roller-coaster ride of revelation, rancor, passion and humor. "Mr. Weller is a bold and productive dramatist." –*NY Times.* [1M, 1W] ISBN: 978-0-8222-2348-1

★ **BECKY'S NEW CAR by Steven Dietz.** Becky Foster is caught in middle age, middle management and in a middling marriage—with no prospects for change on the horizon. Then one night a socially inept and grief-struck millionaire stumbles into the car dealership where Becky works. "Gently and consistently funny." –*Variety.* "Perfect blend of hilarious comedy and substantial weight." –*Broadway Hour.* [4M, 3W] ISBN: 978-0-8222-2393-1

DRAMATISTS PLAY SERVICE, INC.
440 Park Avenue South, New York, NY 10016 212-683-8960 Fax 212-213-1539
postmaster@dramatists.com www.dramatists.com

NEW PLAYS

★ **AT HOME AT THE ZOO by Edward Albee.** Edward Albee delves deeper into his play THE ZOO STORY by adding a first act, HOMELIFE, which precedes Peter's fateful meeting with Jerry on a park bench in Central Park. "An essential and heartening experience." *–NY Times.* "Darkly comic and thrilling." *–Time Out.* "Genuinely fascinating." *–Journal News.* [2M, 1W] ISBN: 978-0-8222-2317-7

★ **PASSING STRANGE book and lyrics by Stew, music by Stew and Heidi Rodewald, created in collaboration with Annie Dorsen.** A daring musical about a young bohemian that takes you from black middle-class America to Amsterdam, Berlin and beyond on a journey towards personal and artistic authenticity. "Fresh, exuberant, bracingly inventive, bitingly funny, and full of heart." *–NY Times.* "The freshest musical in town!" *–Wall Street Journal.* "Excellent songs and a vulnerable heart." *–Variety.* [4M, 3W] ISBN: 978-0-8222-2400-6

★ **REASONS TO BE PRETTY by Neil LaBute.** Greg really, truly adores his girlfriend, Steph. Unfortunately, he also thinks she has a few physical imperfections, and when he mentions them, all hell breaks loose. "Tight, tense and emotionally true." *–Time Magazine.* "Lively and compulsively watchable." *–The Record.* [2M, 2W] ISBN: 978-0-8222-2394-8

★ **OPUS by Michael Hollinger.** With only a few days to rehearse a grueling Beethoven masterpiece, a world-class string quartet struggles to prepare their highest-profile performance ever—a televised ceremony at the White House. "Intimate, intense and profoundly moving." *–Time Out.* "Worthy of scores of bravissimos." *–BroadwayWorld.com.* [4M, 1W] ISBN: 978-0-8222-2363-4

★ **BECKY SHAW by Gina Gionfriddo.** When an evening calculated to bring happiness takes a dark turn, crisis and comedy ensue in this wickedly funny play that asks what we owe the people we love and the strangers who land on our doorstep. "As engrossing as it is ferociously funny." *–NY Times.* "Gionfriddo is some kind of genius." *–Variety.* [2M, 3W] ISBN: 978-0-8222-2402-0

★ **KICKING A DEAD HORSE by Sam Shepard.** Hobart Struther's horse has just dropped dead. In an eighty-minute monologue, he discusses what path brought him here in the first place, the fate of his marriage, his career, politics and eventually the nature of the universe. "Deeply instinctual and intuitive." *–NY Times.* "The brilliance is in the infinite reverberations Shepard extracts from his simple metaphor." *–TheaterMania.* [1M, 1W] ISBN: 978-0-8222-2336-8

DRAMATISTS PLAY SERVICE, INC.
440 Park Avenue South, New York, NY 10016 212-683-8960 Fax 212-213-1539
postmaster@dramatists.com www.dramatists.com

NEW PLAYS

★ **AUGUST: OSAGE COUNTY by Tracy Letts.** WINNER OF THE 2008 PULITZER PRIZE AND TONY AWARD. When the large Weston family reunites after Dad disappears, their Oklahoma homestead explodes in a maelstrom of repressed truths and unsettling secrets. "Fiercely funny and bitingly sad." –*NY Times.* "Ferociously entertaining." –*Variety.* "A hugely ambitious, highly combustible saga." –*NY Daily News.* [6M, 7W] ISBN: 978-0-8222-2300-9

★ **RUINED by Lynn Nottage.** WINNER OF THE 2009 PULITZER PRIZE. Set in a small mining town in Democratic Republic of Congo, RUINED is a haunting, probing work about the resilience of the human spirit during times of war. "A full-immersion drama of shocking complexity and moral ambiguity." –*Variety.* "Sincere, passionate, courageous." –*Chicago Tribune.* [8M, 4W] ISBN: 978-0-8222-2390-0

★ **GOD OF CARNAGE by Yasmina Reza, translated by Christopher Hampton.** WINNER OF THE 2009 TONY AWARD. A playground altercation between boys brings together their Brooklyn parents, leaving the couples in tatters as the rum flows and tensions explode. "Satisfyingly primitive entertainment." –*NY Times.* "Elegant, acerbic, entertainingly fueled on pure bile." –*Variety.* [2M, 2W] ISBN: 978-0-8222-2399-3

★ **THE SEAFARER by Conor McPherson.** Sharky has returned to Dublin to look after his irascible, aging brother. Old drinking buddies Ivan and Nicky are holed up at the house too, hoping to play some cards. But with the arrival of a stranger from the distant past, the stakes are raised ever higher. "Dark and enthralling Christmas fable." –*NY Times.* "A timeless classic." –*Hollywood Reporter.* [5M] ISBN: 978-0-8222-2284-2

★ **THE NEW CENTURY by Paul Rudnick.** When the playwright is Paul Rudnick, expectations are geared for a play both hilarious and smart, and this provocative and outrageous comedy is no exception. "The one-liners fly like rockets." –*NY Times.* "The funniest playwright around." –*Journal News.* [2M, 3W] ISBN: 978-0-8222-2315-3

★ **SHIPWRECKED! AN ENTERTAINMENT—THE AMAZING ADVENTURES OF LOUIS DE ROUGEMONT (AS TOLD BY HIMSELF) by Donald Margulies.** The amazing story of bravery, survival and celebrity that left nineteenth-century England spellbound. Dare to be whisked away. "A deft, literate narrative." –*LA Times.* "Springs to life like a theatrical pop-up book." –*NY Times.* [2M, 1W] ISBN: 978-0-8222-2341-2

DRAMATISTS PLAY SERVICE, INC.
440 Park Avenue South, New York, NY 10016   212-683-8960   Fax 212-213-1539
postmaster@dramatists.com   www.dramatists.com